D0681042

YOUR BEREAVEMENT

YOUR
BEREAVEMENT

By

TALBOT G. MOHAN
Secretary of the Church
Pastoral-Aid Society

HODDER AND STOUGHTON

Printed in Great Britain
for Hodder and Stoughton Ltd.,
St. Paul's House, Warwick Lane, London, E.C.4,
by Richard Clay (The Chaucer Press), Ltd.,
Bungay, Suffolk

Contents

I

PRELIMINARY CONSIDERATIONS

The Christian View of Life and Death

As I was looking through the list of "Deaths" on the front page of *The Times* recently, I saw with a shock the name of a Guards officer who had been killed in an accident. I was grieved for his parents, for he was a young fellow of great promise. Educated at Eton and Sandhurst, he appeared to be destined for a great career in the Army, in which both his father and his grandfather had given distinguished service. It seemed such a tragic waste of a splendid young life. I wrote a letter of sympathy to his father, and knowing how devoted his parents were to their only son, it was hard to find words of comfort. In his reply he said something to this effect, "We are able to rejoice. I know you will understand what I mean."

What he meant was that, for the Christian, death is not a tragedy but a triumphant entrance into a fuller life. Perhaps this puzzles you? You cannot conceive how anyone could find joy in disaster? It may be that you have lost a beloved husband, or wife, or child, or parent, or friend. Life seems empty and meaningless. You cannot think how the future is to be faced. He or she has meant so much to you; you have been bound up with one another, and now it seems as if part of you has gone for ever and the future is blank and dark and terrible. It is to try to help you that this book has been written. Its aim is that you should discover the secret which will enable you to rejoice, though at present the thought of joy is farthest from your mind.

If we could talk together, you would probably say something like this, "If only I knew whether there is a life after death, and what has happened to my beloved. If only the veil could be drawn aside, that I could get a glimpse into the unknown. One moment my loved one was with me—the next he was gone. I wish I could be sure; but it is like facing a blank wall; no one knows and no one can tell. That is the bitterness of it!" Yes, that indeed is bitter.

HOW CAN WE KNOW ABOUT THE FUTURE?

The purpose of this book is to assure you that the future is not unknown, that we *can* know what happens to us after death and that we can be sure. But, you say, where is this knowledge to be found? There is, of course, only one source, and that is God Himself. God sent His Son into the world to live and die as a man. What Jesus told His contemporaries about the future life is recorded in the Bible. There is also there recorded further information, given us through those who were inspired by God to convey to us the mind of God, the purpose of God, and the will of God for men and women. We accept the Bible as the authentic word of God to man. If we reject its evidence, there is no other; there can be no other.

This is not the place to argue the authority of the Bible. We can only beg you to investigate it for yourself and to believe that its authority has been recognised all through the ages and is the basis of our faith as members of the Church of England to-day. You will find this stated in the Articles of our Faith, set forth in the Prayer Book: "Holy Scripture containeth all things necessary to salvation: so that whatsoever is not read therein, nor may be proved thereby, is not to be required of any man that it should be believed as an article of the faith" (Article VI). We would add for

your comfort that the authority of the Bible has been
proved over and over again by countless men and
women who have found that, when they have accepted
its promises and acted upon them, God vindicates His
word in their experience. You are invited to take God
at His word.

In the Christian view this life is a probation; death is
the horizon beyond which life stretches away into
eternity. The Christian does not think of life as
bounded by death, as a long or short experience during
which he grows in knowledge and in stature, achieves
success or failure in his calling or occupation, and then
declines in physical and mental power until at last life
fades out and that is the end. To him life is a pilgrimage.
He is a stranger here, his citizenship is in heaven.

"We've no abiding city here,
    This may distress the worldling's mind;
But will not cost the saint a tear
    Who hopes a better rest to find."

LIVING IN THE LIGHT OF ETERNITY

Thus the Christian view of death is changed by the
knowledge that life is eternal because our Lord Jesus
has triumphed over death. St. Paul cries out with
exultation, "O death, where is thy sting? O grave, where
is thy victory? The sting of death is sin and the strength
of sin is the law, but thanks be to God which giveth us
the victory through our Lord Jesus Christ" (1 Cor. 15.
55–57). Death is bound to bring sorrow, but "we sorrow
not as others which have no hope". Death is bound to
bring loss, but "our light affliction, which is but for a
moment, worketh for us a far more exceeding and
eternal weight of glory". Death marks the end of our
earthly pilgrimage and the opening of the gates into the
City of God.

It is not easy in these days to live in the light of

eternity. So much which helps to make life happy and comfortable is found in our high standard of living, in the material benefits which modern invention has given us in such rich measure. New vistas of untold enjoyment stretch out before us so that the hopes of many people are concentrated on material progress. This is a pity, because life, even if it reaches or surpasses the allotted span, is as a moment of time in relation to eternity. If we could grasp the significance of this, we should readjust our values, we should see things in a proper perspective, and we should cease to regard this world as our goal and this life as the limit of our happiness.

Lord Inman has said that when he was Chairman of the B.B.C. he was surprised how rarely broadcast sermons and addresses dealt with the subject of life after death. He was informed by the then Director of Religious Broadcasting that he had read over 6,000 addresses and only one dealt with the future life. He recalls that a favourite hymn of his boyhood days was "I'm but a stranger here, heaven is my home". If we were all assured that we should be reunited with our loved ones beyond the grave, how eagerly we should look forward to meeting them; how avidly we should study and seek out all there was to be discovered about that glorious prospect! In the following chapters we shall try to give the Christian answer to the questions which so many are asking. Is there a life after death? Shall we see our loved ones again? Where are those who have died? What will the future life be like? Is there really a resurrection of the dead?

What Evidence is there of Life After Death?

GALLUP POLLS and mass observation have shown that a startling proportion of people—and among them churchgoers—declare that they do not believe in a future life. But we may be allowed to question whether this view is the result of serious consideration or is, in fact, simply an acknowledgment that they have never given it any thought. There is a good deal of evidence to suggest that deep down in the heart of "everyman" is an uneasy belief that there will be a day of reckoning and that, in some way which he does not understand, the kind of life he lives here will determine his future destiny. He may even deny that he has any such thoughts, but they come to the surface in times of crisis. Does not this universal subconscious conviction of coming judgment carry with it the implication of survival, at least for those who are successful in escaping condemnation?

We live in an age when the most incredible secrets of nature are being revealed, which were undreamed of by our grandfathers. We have unleashed mighty forces which are frightening in their fearful potential for destruction. New wonders of the universe are revealed by modern devices which are able to pierce far beyond the distances which our telescopes have hitherto reached.

It is often asserted that in the light of these stupendous discoveries man is seen in a very small perspective, and therefore it is foolish to think of him any longer as being important enough to merit survival. But this is to ignore the fact that these wonders would never have been known had not man been able to discover them and harness them for his own use. Not all scientists are obsessed with the view that the size and complexity of the universe are an argument against the Christian faith. One, whose sphere of research is aerodynamics and who may be seen and heard on television speaking about space-travel, told the writer that he marvelled, not so much at the wonders which scientific discovery revealed, as at the wisdom and power of their Creator and Sustainer. The Christian believes that the Creator is also the essence of the supreme quality of Love. C. S. Lewis writes, "If it is maintained that anything so small as the Earth must, in any event, be too unimportant to merit the love of the Creator, we reply that no Christian ever supposed we did merit it. Christ did not die for men because they were intrinsically worth dying for, but because He is intrinsically love, and therefore loves infinitely. And what, after all, does the *size* of a world or a creature tell us about its 'importance' or value?"

SURVIVAL IS CONSISTENT WITH GOD'S CHARACTER

Is it consistent with God's character to suppose that the "crown" of His creation is finally subject to a useless and meaningless extinction? We are told that matter is ultimately indestructible. If this is true of man's body, might we not expect it to be equally true of his soul? If God is a God of love, it is unthinkable that the revelation of His attitude to man should not include His desire for man's immortality. It is equally incredible that God should have sent His Son Jesus Christ into the world to live and die for men if they are destined for a grave of eternal forgetfulness. "If in this life only we have hope in Christ", says St. Paul, "we are of all men most miserable" (1 Cor. 15. 19).

It is not, however, upon argument about either man's nature or God's character that the Christian bases his hope of a future life, but upon the revelation we have received in Holy Scripture. What, then, does the Bible tell us?

The Bible tells us that death is like a "sleep" from which we shall awake. Jesus said of Lazarus, the brother of Mary of Bethany, "Our friend Lazarus sleepeth". To the puzzled disciples who thought He referred to normal sleep He said plainly, "Lazarus is dead". The friends of Jairus, the Jewish ruler, laughed Jesus to scorn when He said of his daughter, "The maid is not dead but sleepeth" (John 11. 11; Matt. 9. 24). Many other references could be quoted which indicate that those who had died were considered to have "fallen asleep". If death is the final extinction of life, it could not conceivably be spoken of as sleep.

The Bible also teaches that death is not the worst thing which can happen to us, because death affects only the body. The body is not the most important part of our being. The Lord Jesus told us to be afraid, not of those who can kill the body, but of those who can kill the soul. The loss of physical life is not comparable to the loss of our souls. Jesus called the rich farmer, whose sole concern was to improve his standard of living, a fool, because with death lurking round the corner, he was planning for limitless material enjoyment. The body is like a dwelling-house. "If our earthly house of this tabernacle were dissolved," says St. Paul, "we have a building of God, a house not made with hands, eternal in the heavens" (2 Cor. 5. 1). Therefore we need not fear the dissolution of the body, because the soul—the true self—is not extinguished by death. If there is no life beyond the grave, we might be justified in giving ourselves up wholly to make the

B

best of this life, but when our Lord advises us not to lay up treasure on earth but in heaven, He implies that there must be an opportunity to enjoy it there. This, surely, is why, though He never refused to heal the body, He was more concerned about the healing of the soul.

THE ETERNAL VALUE OF MAN'S SOUL

The infinite value to God of man's soul is seen in some of our Lord's parables, for example that of the Lost Sheep. The Shepherd is not content that 99 per cent. of his sheep are safe in the fold. He searches the mountains tirelessly till he finds the one lost sheep, and he rejoices more over that sheep than over all the others. This parable, and those of the Lost Coin and the Prodigal Son, all illustrate the joy of heaven over one repentant sinner. But what would be the reason for that joy, if the sinner is to die eternally when this life ends? Why did our Lord say that He gave His life for the sheep if there is no future for them? Why did our Lord place such a high value on the human soul if its existence is so fleeting?

There are other clear indications of the Biblical assumption of a future life which we shall consider in more detail later. I need only draw attention to two of them. First, there is the fact of judgment of which the New Testament has so much to say, and to which Jesus referred in many of His parables. He tells us that there is a time coming when those who are in the grave will come forth, "they that have done good unto the resurrection of life and they that have done evil to the resurrection of condemnation" (John 5. 29). If there is no life after death what is the purpose of judgment? Neither reward nor punishment would be possible.

Secondly, a favourite theme in the New Testament is everlasting life. We are told how we may enter into that life. We shall notice a firm note of certainty which should remove any lingering doubt as to the possibility of knowing anything about the life to come. Let me give you a few of the many statements on the subject with their references, so that you may verify them for yourselves. Our Lord declared that He Himself was "the way" to the Father, and that those who believe His word have everlasting life "and shall not come into judgment". He promised the thief who died beside Him on the cross that he should be with Him "to-day" in paradise. Those who believe in Christ are exhorted not to grieve over the dead as others do who have no hope, but to take comfort from the promise that in the new life beyond the grave "God shall wipe away all tears . . . and there shall be no more death" (John 14. 6; 12. 36; Luke 23. 43; 1 Thess. 4. 13; Rev. 15. 17).

I hope I have said enough to convince you that it is impossible not to believe in a life after death, unless we reject the clear teaching of God's word and insist upon a pessimistic attitude which refuses to be convinced by either reason or revelation. Let us now go on to try to answer some questions about the future life.

II

FUNDAMENTAL QUESTIONS

— 3 —

Where are Our Beloved Dead ?

WE now come to the very core of our subject, to that which we all long to know. Where are our loved ones? What is their condition? Are they conscious?

Of the fundamental fact of survival God has left us in no doubt. There is ample revelation of His love for us, of His desire that men should be redeemed and dwell with Him for ever, and of the costly way by wh ich He made his possible. He has told us much about the provision He has made for us in the life to come; that we shall dwell with Him, that we shall be delivered from sin, freed from pain and sorrow, and united with those who have gone before us in Christ. We know that we shall serve Him and spend eternity learning to know Him more perfectly. He has told us enough to remove all uncertainty and to give us joyful assurance.

Of course there is much more that we should like to know, but for reasons best known to Himself He has not seen fit to reveal more than is necessary to convince us that "in Christ" all is well with our loved ones. The temptation to speculate about details which, however interesting, are not essential for us to know, should be firmly resisted. It is idle and profitless. It leads on inevitably to dabbling in cults which can only bring sorrow and disillusion. The Bible warns us againt the age-old methods of prying into the unknown, and forbids them in no uncertain terms. Spiritism, divination, wizardry, and necromancy were all condemned very early in the history of God's dealings with men. We

21

are told that "all that do these things are an abomi-
nation unto the Lord" (Deut. 18. 12). There is the
pathetic story of King Saul, who had cleansed the
national life by putting away those who had "familiar
spirits", yet in the closing days of his disappointing
career betook himself to the woman of Endor with
disastrous results. The temptation to resort to any
means which promise contact with our loved ones may
be overwhelming to some and especially to those who
have no hope in Christ. But it is a path across which
is written in flaming letters: "DANGER—KEEP OUT".
Rudyard Kipling, in the story of his much-travelled life,
says, "I have seen too much evil and sorrow and wreck
of good minds on the road to Endor to take one step
along that perilous track".[1]

Let us be content with what God has revealed, and
when we long to know what is hidden from our sight
remember that our minds could not grasp the reality; it
would be impossible to find either words or means
capable of conveying the whole truth to our limited
understanding. It is sufficient to be assured that, "Eye
hath not seen, nor ear heard, neither have entered into
the heart of man, the things which God hath prepared
for them that love Him" (1 Cor. 2. 9).

"AT HOME" WITH THE LORD

Let us now try to answer the question—what happens
to us when we die? The body, we know, remains—but
without life, inert, motionless, unresponsive. The real
"person", the soul which inhabited the body, has gone.
Where? We have remarked that the Bible frequently
speaks of death as sleep. But sleep appears to refer to
the *body*, not to the soul. Our Lord on the cross told
the penitent thief, "To-day shalt thou be with me in
paradise", while on the Mount of Transfiguration

[1] *Something of Myself*, p. 215.

Moses and Elijah appeared and talked with Jesus (Luke 23. 43; 9. 30). Both these references imply consciousness and activity. They could hardly be consistent with the view that the dead are lost in unconscious sleep until the resurrection morning. St. Paul writes in his Second Epistle to the Corinthians that he has no fear of death, or the separation from the body which this will involve, because to be "at home" in his earthly body is to be absent from the Lord. He therefore even prefers death, for he is "willing rather to be absent from the body, and to be 'at home' with the Lord". St. Paul again shows his confidence concerning the condition which immediately follows death, in his letter to the Philippians. He confesses to being on the horns of a dilemma, having a desire to die and "to be with Christ, which is far better", and yet being anxious not to desert them in their need. For him, therefore, death is not a disaster but a positive gain (see 2 Cor. 5; Phil. 1).

This all seems to imply that the soul of the believer, after it has left the body, is in the *conscious* enjoyment of that happy condition which we call "with Christ". We ought, however, to say that many Christians find it difficult to conceive of a "disembodied" spirit enjoying an existence of any kind, though they would be the first to admit that this difficulty may be conditioned entirely by their own human limitations. They find a possible solution of the problem in the Biblical statement that "one day is with the Lord as a thousand years, and a thousand years as one day". Time is a human conception and presents no limitation in the mind of God. Thus there may, in fact, be no gap between death and resurrection except in our earth-bound imagination.[1]

But where is "with Christ"? Is it a place? The Bible

---

[1] A "Fact and Faith" film, produced under the direction of the Moody Bible Institute, entitled "Time and Eternity" presents some interesting scientific evidence which enables us to begin to perceive dimly the possibility of a timeless existence.

appears to leave us in no doubt about this. It speaks of God's dwelling-place as heaven. Jesus, we are told, ascended into heaven. Stephen, at his death as the first Christian martyr, looked up steadfastly towards heaven and "saw Jesus". Our Lord exhorts us to lay up treasure in heaven rather than on earth. St. Peter writes of "an inheritance reserved in heaven". The writer of the Epistle to the Hebrews declares that Christ entered "into heaven itself, now to appear in the presence of God for us" (Acts 1. 11; 7. 56; Matt. 19. 21; 1 Pet. 1. 4; Heb. 9. 24). The conception of heaven as a place has been accepted by the Church throughout the centuries. In the light of the numerous references in the Scriptures which it is difficult to explain away, it is hard to believe that the Church could have been wrong. It is sometimes suggested that heaven is "a state of mind". It would be impossible on this hypothesis to explain what happened to our Lord's glorified resurrection body when He ascended into heaven. That body was certainly not a ghost or a spirit, for it could be seen and touched, and it was capable of eating. Our Church believes that He ascended into heaven "with flesh, bones, and all things appertaining to the perfection of man's nature" (Article IV). It surely demands a "place" for the home of anything so substantial as a body. To "spiritualise" heaven is a symptom of an age which has largely lost the hope of everlasting life and is so obsessed by materialistic conceptions that it cannot conceive of heaven as anything other than a pleasant ecclesiastical dream.

A NEW CREATION

Nevertheless there is to be found in Scripture that which warns us not to press the human analogy of a "place" too far. "Heaven . . . cannot contain Him", said Solomon. And Isaiah writes, "Thus saith the

Lord, the heaven is my throne, and the earth is my footstool" (2 Chron. 2. 6; Isa. 66. 1). While therefore there is nothing to discourage us from believing that heaven is a place, and everything to encourage us, yet we must remember that our limited experience makes it impossible for us to integrate perfectly the spiritual and the material. In our world they dwell in watertight compartments. We set one over against the other. The explanation perhaps lies in a New Creation, of which, possibly, we are given a glimpse in our Lord's risen Body; a Creation which unites perfectly and inseparably the spiritual and the spacial without involving any limitation of the power and majesty of God. Therefore we are quite right to rejoice in the belief that heaven is a place, as spiritual as anything we have wished in our most exalted moments and as satisfying as our physical experiences could desire.

Calvin comments, "As our gross minds are unable to conceive of His ineffable glory, it is designated to us by 'heaven' ". We are assured that those who fall asleep in Jesus are "with Christ", which is all we need to know and is enough to fill us with thanksgiving. Perhaps the veil between us is far thinner than we think; the appearance of Moses and Elijah on the Mount of Transfiguration makes this seem very probable.

There is a further question concerning the blessed dead which we must all have asked. How much do they know about our present condition? Are they aware of our joys and sorrows? Can they follow the course of our spiritual struggles or our progress in material matters? It is not possible to answer with certainty, for Holy Scripture gives us no evidence which puts the matter beyond dispute. There is a passage in the Epistle to the Hebrews which is often assumed to mean that the saints are watching our progress with the deepest concern. "Wherefore seeing we also are compassed about with so great a cloud of witnesses, let us lay aside every weight, and the sin which doth so easily beset us, and let us run with patience the race that is set before us, looking unto Jesus. . . ." (Heb. 12. 1–2). The picture in the mind of the writer is obviously that of the public games. He sees the vast crowd of spectators rising tier upon tier in the amphitheatre; the runners with their eyes fixed upon the goal and yet seeing, as in a cloud, a great array of faces. This seems to be conclusive; but saints and scholars have never been quite sure, for the following reasons. First, they are agreed that the chief thought in the writer's mind is "looking unto Jesus". *He* is the goal upon which the contestants' gaze is concentrated. Secondly, the word "witnesses" ("so great a cloud of witnesses") does not mean "spectators", although the conception appears logical. The reference is rather to the *witness* of the heroes of faith enumerated in the previous chapter. It may then be that the writer, having given us an impressive list of the great saints of the past who have preceded us in the "race", does no more than ask us to remember and be encouraged by their witness. But this does not explain the expression "compassed about", which could reasonably imply that they are watching us with deep concern. Thus we are left with no certain conviction that the saints in glory are cognisant of our welfare. There are some reasons why we might shrink from the thought that they are, for then they must often be grieved by our failures and misfortunes. That would appear to contradict the satisfying belief that they are in joy and felicity where there is neither pain nor tears. We must be content to accept the answer, that we cannot tell if or how much they know of our life here on earth, and to comfort ourselves with the incontrovertible truth of our Saviour's full knowledge and loving care.

NEED WE PRAY FOR THE DEAD?

It is in the light of what we have just been saying about the happy state of those who have died in the faith of Christ that we must consider whether we should pray for them. Do they need our prayers? What can our prayers achieve?

In this, as in all else, we should be guided by Holy Scripture. The Bible is silent on the subject.[1] But it is not silent about the condition of those who have finished their earthly life. The Scripture everywhere implies that we determine our own eternal destiny in this life; there is nothing to encourage us to believe that prayers can influence that destiny after death. Those who have died without any profession of faith in Christ we must therefore leave to the tender mercy and justice of a Saviour whose love for them is far greater than our own.

So, also, the evidence is overwhelming that those who have died in the faith of Jesus Christ are with Him, purified from sin and delivered from "the burden of the flesh". What, then, can our prayers accomplish? Is it not incongruous that we, struggling against the temptations of our sinful nature and subject to the limitations and hindrances of mortality, should pray for those who are in joy and felicity, and whose strivings have been crowned with the gift of immortality?

Thus many branches of the Christian Church share with our own the belief that to pray for the dead is to contradict our faith in the assurance of that eternal life, which is the essence of the Gospel. The compilers of our Prayer Book excluded such prayers, because they

---

[1] It has been suggested that St. Paul's words about Onesiphorus in 2 Tim. 1. 18, "The Lord grant unto him that he may find mercy of the Lord in that day" is a prayer for the departed. But it is nowhere stated that Onesiphorus was dead. It seems much more likely that some commentators are projecting into this statement a meaning which it does not bear.

involved the assumption of Purgatory, a state which has no warrant in Holy Scripture and is described in our Articles as "vainly invented".

Instead, the Prayer Book provides us with thanksgiving for the earthly life and present bliss of the departed, and for their example which we are exhorted to follow. We say, for instance, at the end of the prayer for the Church Militant in our Communion Service: "We also bless thy holy Name for all thy servants departed this life in thy faith and fear; beseeching thee to give us grace so to follow their good examples, that with them we may be partakers of thy heavenly kingdom: Grant this, O Father, for Jesus Christ's sake, our only Mediator and Advocate. Amen."

We believe it wise to follow the example of our Church, that is, to accept the extreme reticence of Holy Scripture and to be content with the assurance it gives of the eternal welfare of those who have died in Christ.

4

What is the Resurrection of the Dead ?

WHEN we recite the Creed each Sunday, we declare our belief "in the resurrection of the body". In our highly scientific age there are some Christians who find it difficult to believe in a resurrection of the *body*, because they suppose that it involves the recovery of the identical particles of matter which were laid in the grave. While this would not be beyond the power of God to accomplish, yet there is no reason to think that it is necessary. The substance of our bodies is constantly being renewed during our lifetime. As Professor C. S. Lewis says, "We all live in second-hand suits".

While therefore we cannot explain how God is able to raise the dead, nevertheless it is certain that a resurrection must be that of the body, because the soul is not laid in the grave; it leaves the body at death.

St. Paul helps us with this very problem by using the analogy of a seed sown in the ground to illustrate the difference between our present physical body and the body we shall receive at the resurrection. "Thou sowest not that body that shall be . . . but God giveth it a body." Whereas the old body was subject to decay, the new body will be immortal; whereas the old may have been infirm or imperfect, the new will be without blemish; whereas the old was subject to many limitations, the resurrection body will be possessed of new powers. It is no longer a physical body but a spiritual body. Mortal flesh cannot inherit the kingdom of God; it must become immortal. That is indeed what will happen to both the dead and the living at the resurrection. St. Paul takes us into his confidence. "Behold I show you a mystery; we shall not all sleep, but we shall all be changed, in a moment, in the twinkling of an eye, at the last trump; . . . the dead shall be raised incorruptible, and we shall be changed" (1 Cor. 15. 37–52).

Of course there are recorded instances of dead persons being raised to life again. Jesus brought back to life the son of the widow of Nain, the daughter of Jairus, Lazarus, and others whose names are not given. Peter commanded Tabitha to arise, and Paul lifted up the dead Eutychus and restored him to life (Luke 7. 14; 8. 45; John 11. 44; Matt. 11. 5; Acts 9. 45; 20. 12). These are not, however, "resurrections" in the strict sense, because the dead took again their natural bodies and resumed normal life. Nevertheless, they do reveal the power of God and are prophetic both of our Lord's resurrection and of ours; though the pattern and mode of our resurrection are to be found not in these "resuscitations" but in the rising again of our Lord Jesus Christ which led to a new plane of existence, as we shall now see.

THE RESURRECTION OF JESUS

Let us then look at His resurrection. He was perfect man. He had a human body like our own. When He died, His body was embalmed and laid in a tomb. On the first Easter morning the disciples came to the tomb and found it empty, but they saw that the grave clothes lay undisturbed as they appeared when they enclosed the body of Jesus. It was obvious that His body had passed through the grave clothes and the sealed tomb. That He had taken His body again is also clear from the fact that He appeared in human form first to Mary and then on many occasions to the other disciples.

But the resurrection had effected a change in His

body. It was no longer subject to the limitations of a physical body. It had passed through the grave clothes and the sealed tomb and was able also to pass through closed doors. When He walked with the two disciples from Jerusalem to Emmaus they did not immediately recognise Him.

Yet it was still in some sense a physical body; Mary was able to hold Him by the feet; the disciples were invited to "Handle me and see, for a spirit hath not flesh and bones as ye see me have". Thomas was commanded "Reach hither thy hand and thrust it into my side". Jesus Himself demonstrated His ability to eat food. When He left the earth to return to His Father the disciples watched Him ascend in bodily form and disappear out of sight in the clouds. We believe that the Lord ascended into heaven with His perfect human nature. We may remember a statement on our Prayer Book, found at the end of the Order for Holy Communion—"The actual Body and Blood of our Saviour Christ are in Heaven, and not here".

OUR RESURRECTION

What proof is there that God will raise us from the dead as He did Jesus? Our Lord's assurances about resurrection are too frequent to record here. Let me remind you of two. When the Sadducees, who did not believe in a resurrection, presented Him with what they thought was an unanswerable argument against it, He reminded them of the word of God written in Exodus 3. 6, "I am the God of Abraham, and the God of Isaac, and the God of Jacob", and added, "God is not the God of the dead, but of the living" (Matt. 22. 32). Again, we have our Lord's specific promise that it was His Father's will that everyone who believed in Him should have everlasting life; "and I will raise him up at the last day" (John 6. 40 and

54). His resurrection provides not only the guarantee but also the prototype of our own. We have seen that His resurrection body was a changed body. It was no longer subject to the limitations which bound it before the Crucifixion. St. Paul, in his letter to the Philippians, gives us the startling information that our bodies will pass through a similar change. His body will provide the pattern for ours. "The body of our humiliation will be made like unto His glorious body" (Phil 3. 21).

The fact of our Lord's resurrection was so vividly fixed in the minds of the Apostles that it became the central point of their teaching. They based their claims concerning Jesus Christ upon it. Over and over again the burden of their preaching was "You killed the Prince of life, whom God hath raised from the dead; whereof we are witnesses". It is particularly noticeable in Acts 10. 40, where Peter once more points to the evidence of the resurrection, saying that God "shewed Him openly" and that the Apostles not only saw Him but "did eat and drink with Him after He rose from the dead". Paul, preaching to the Thessalonians, showed that it was necessary for Christ to die and to rise again from the dead, "and this Jesus whom I preach unto you, is Christ" (Acts 17. 3).

The Apostles not only based their teaching upon the resurrection, but also went on to claim that it was a guarantee of our resurrection. There is an example of this in Paul's first letter to the Corinthians. He has been describing the appalling plight of mankind if, as some of his contemporaries had argued, there was no resurrection. He then proceeds to describe our Lord's resurrection as the first-fruits of a great harvest. Every Hebrew would understand the allusion. We read in the Book of Leviticus of a Divine command to offer the first-fruits of every harvest to God. The offering was an acknowledgment that they owed everything to Him.

It was, too, a representative gift in which was dedicated the whole harvest. The gathering of the first-fruits was also, for them, a promise of the fuller harvest yet to come. The custom had continued to be celebrated annually and would have been due to take place near the time of our Lord's resurrection. It may be that St. Paul had this in mind when he describes Christ as the "first fruits of them that slept" (1 Cor. 15. 20). His resurrection was the guarantee of the resurrection of the dead.

ETERNAL LIFE A PRESENT POSSESSION

Nevertheless we do not have to wait for the resurrection in order to enjoy resurrection life. Jesus is quite specific in His teaching on this. He announced that everyone who received His message and believed in God's offer through Him had everlasting life already. The Father and the Son were one in the great work of redemption. Those who accept what Jesus has accomplished for us receive immediately (if we may use the metaphor again) the first-fruits of the greater harvest to come. We are united with Christ and cannot therefore be separated from Him even by death (John 5. 24). St. Paul draws the obvious conclusion that if we share His life, we should share His interests. Our affection should be set upon heavenly rather than earthly things. Our treasure is in heaven and our hearts will be there also (Col. 3. 1-2). St. Paul goes even farther, and speaking of himself says that he no longer lives, but Christ lives in him (Gal. 2. 20). If Christ dwells within us He will show Himself through our lives, manifesting the truth of the claim that resurrection life can be communicated during our lifetime through the power of the risen Saviour.

It is an exciting and thrilling experience to reach a conviction that eternal life is assured in Christ Jesus. It enables us to understand St. Peter's exclamation,

"Blessed be the God and Father of our Lord Jesus Christ, which according to His abundant mercy hath begotten us again unto a lively hope by the resurrection of Jesus Christ from the dead" (1 Pet. 1. 3). This living hope is likened to an anchor for the soul. The illustration is drawn from the practice of Galilean fishermen, who fastened an anchor ashore and then fished offshore, knowing that in the darkness or in fog they had only to haul on the anchor to reach safety. The Christian hope is an anchor which reaches beyond the veil which separates us from the unseen world. Our anchor is both "sure and steadfast" (Heb. 6. 19).

A CONVINCING GUARANTEE

It is this sure and steadfast hope of eternal life which constitutes the triumph of the Gospel. The gospels record that the ministry of Jesus Christ fulfilled an Old Testament prophecy. Light had come to those who dwelt in darkness. Many to-day are still in darkness and the fear of death. To them the good news comes that Jesus has brought life and immortality to light through the Gospel. They need no longer live in uncertainty, because Jesus took our nature upon Him and passed through death to bring us life. The writer of the Epistle to the Hebrews declares that the purpose of His coming thus to share our life was also to share our death and destroy its power, and so set us free from the tyranny with which so many are bound by the fear of death (Heb. 2. 14–15). Christ has conquered death, removed its sting, and given us the victory. He holds the key; our safety and security are in His hand. The assurance of life is offered to us, but it requires action on our part. That offer should be accepted lest the opportunity be lost. There is a warning to which we should take heed—"how shall we escape, if we neglect so great salvation?" (Heb. 2. 3).

5

What Events are Associated with
the Resurrection ?

THERE is general agreement on the two main events associated with the resurrection, namely that the return of Christ will precede it and that judgment will follow it. We shall confine ourselves to these two facts.

THE COMING AGAIN OF JESUS CHRIST

First, then, the return of Jesus Christ. The Church has throughout its history believed that the Lord Jesus will return in person to this earth. We admit this truth Sunday by Sunday when we recite the Apostles' Creed, "He shall come to judge the quick and the dead". As with other vital Scriptural truths, there have been times when the Church's vision of this great hope has been dimmed. We have been passing through such a period when it was thought to be rather naïve to believe in the literal coming again of Jesus Christ. To-day there is a revival of interest in eschatology (the doctrine of the "last things"), and it is acknowledged that such an event is a fitting climax to history and a momentous happening with which to usher in the timeless reign of our Lord Jesus Christ.

There is a solid basis of fact for this belief, both in the assurance given us by Christ Himself, and in the consistent teaching of the New Testament as a whole. The "blessed hope" is seen from so many angles, and related to so much which determines our welfare and our destiny, that we cannot eliminate it without

wrecking the plan and purpose of God as revealed to us
in Scripture. Thus it is offered as a consolation in times
of depression or discouragement. When our Lord was
about to leave His disciples He begged them not to
allow their hearts to be troubled or to be afraid—He
was going to prepare a place for them, "and", He said,
"if I go and prepare a place for you, I will come again,
and receive you unto myself; that where I am, there ye
may be also" (John 14. 3). After the Ascension of Jesus
into heaven, and while the disciples were still gazing
intently at the cloud into which He had disappeared,
two men in white apparel appeared in their midst and
assured them that He would return again in the same
manner as they had seen Him depart (Acts 1. 9–11).
They were so confident of the authenticity of this word
of comfort that they returned to Jerusalem, not dejected,
as might have been supposed, but with great joy. Like-
wise, St. Paul, writing to the Thessalonians who had
suffered bereavement, comforts them with the assurance
of our Lord's return and their loved ones' simultaneous
resurrection (1 Thess. 4. 13–18). These first Christians
were joyfully "looking for that blessed hope, and the
glorious appearing of the great God and our Saviour
Jesus Christ" (Titus 2. 13).

Our Lord's teaching related His own return to the
end of this age, and there is always a note of finality and
urgency in His words—urgency that we should be prepared for this event and finality because, if we are found
unprepared, there is no indication that the opportunity
will recur. On one occasion the disciples asked Jesus
privately what would be the sign of His coming and of
the "end of the world". Our Lord's long and detailed
reply is to be found in chapters 24 and 25 of St.
Matthew's Gospel. There is much here that is difficult
to understand and to interpret, but an indelible impression remains after reading this reply and comparing
it with other New Testament teaching. The exact time

of the Advent is not revealed; it will be sudden, as instantaneous as a flash of lightning, and as unexpected as a thief in the night. As the warnings by Noah of the coming flood were ignored, so Christ's coming will find the world as a whole heedless and unprepared. To the disciples He urges a sense of responsibility and stewardship combined with a readiness to give an immediate account. This is illustrated in the parables of the faithful and unfaithful servants, of the talents, and of the wise and foolish virgins. For those who are ready and watching, the Lord's return will be a joyful event. Frances Ridley Havergal has immortalised the thrill of it in her moving hymn:

> "O the joy to see Thee reigning,
>   Thee, mine own beloved Lord,
> Every tongue Thy Name confessing,
>   Worship, honour, glory, blessing,
> Brought to Thee with one accord;
>   Thee my Master and my Friend,
> Vindicated and enthroned,
>   Unto earth's remotest end
> Glorified, adored and owned."

Everything points to the fact that the moment of our Lord's coming will be a stupendous event, transcending history and defying description. It was His claim before the Council that they would see Him sitting on the right hand of power and coming in the clouds of heaven, which horrified the High Priest by its startling and tremendous implication, and led to His immediate condemnation to death for blasphemy (Matt. 26. 64). St. Paul tells us that He "shall descend from heaven with a shout, with the voice of the archangel and with the trump of God" (1 Thess. 4. 16). His coming therefore will be visible and audible throughout the whole world.

The Advent of the King will be the signal for the resurrection. The Scripture says very simply that the Lord will gather together His elect from the four winds.

The dead in Christ shall rise first, being given resurrection bodies. The bodies of the living will pass through the change which is necessary to fit them for the heavenly sphere, and we shall then together be caught up "to meet the Lord in the air: and so shall we ever be with the Lord" (Matt. 24. 31; 1 Thess. 4. 16; 1 Cor. 15. 42–44; 1 Cor. 15. 52; 1 Thess. 4. 17). How simple and yet how breathtaking! To the unbeliever it sounds crazy, but to those who are prepared to take God at His word He gives conviction which no human agency can impart, that this is true and that death will be swallowed up in victory.

If this looks crude in cold print, the reality will be unspeakably solemn, majestic, and awe-inspiring, a perfect manifestation of the power and wisdom of God. Modern scientific discovery helps us to overcome any reluctance we may have in believing it to be possible. You would have been incredulous had you lived one hundred years ago, and been told that men would one day fly in the sky at more than one thousand miles per hour; that one would be able to hear in one's own room a voice speaking on the other side of the world as clearly as if it was in the room, and yet with no visible connection to account for it; that we should be able to sit comfortably at home and watch a football match in progress one hundred miles away; that we should look into the sky and see a man-made earth-satellite making its swift journey round and round the globe. All these "miracles" have been made possible through the ingenuity of man harnessing the hitherto undiscovered wonders of God's creation. Are we prepared to ascribe to man more wisdom than we give to his Creator?

THE JUDGMENT

The first great fact, then, upon which there is general agreement is that the resurrection is preceded by the return in glory of the Lord Jesus Christ. The second is that the judgment will follow the resurrection. We approach this subject with great reluctance, for it is one from which we naturally shrink. But it would be unfaithful not to face it, and we must seek to do so with great tenderness, using only such plainness of speech as did our Saviour Himself, and setting forth His lovingkindness and mercy which will have all men to be saved and to come to the knowledge of the truth.

It is quite impossible not to be impressed by the teaching of our Lord which linked His coming with judgment. True it is, that for the Christian the dominant note of the Advent season is joy in the prospect of His return; yet the thought of judgment is there. The hymn.

> "Lo He comes with clouds descending,
> Once for favoured sinners slain"

echoes, of course, the words of Revelation 1. 7: "Behold, he cometh with clouds; and every eye shall see him, and they also which pierced him: and all kindreds of the earth shall wail because of him." We must all stand before the judgment seat, small and great, rich and poor, high or humble.

The scene is pictured by St. John the Divine as he saw it in his vision. The Judge sat upon a great white throne. The sight was such that the "earth and the heaven fled away" from the face of Him that sat on the throne (Rev. 20. 12). The books were opened—the record of men's deeds—and the dead were judged by those things which were written in the books, according to their works.

Among those who stand before the judgment seat are the wilful and deliberate wrong-doers who, "knowing the judgment of God, that they which commit such things are worthy of death, not only do the same, but have pleasure in them that do them" (Rom. 1. 32). St.

Paul describes them as "inexcusable", despising the forbearance and longsuffering of God which is intended to lead them to repentance, and determined to treasure up for themselves the righteous judgment of God. We may think that these do not deserve pity because they have deliberately counted the cost and must be prepared to pay. But God has more pity for them than have we. He has no pleasure in the death of the sinner. Indeed, because of His great love He has gone to the utmost length to secure their pardon and safety. Yet if men insist upon rejecting life and choosing death, they declare their own judgment. If we persist in rebellion against God and spurn His love after we have received the offer of His peace and pardon, then "there remaineth no more sacrifice for sins, but a certain fearful looking for of judgment" (Heb. 10. 26).

Then there are those who might be described as "the heathen"; primitive peoples who live in the remote places of the earth and have never heard the Gospel or seen a Bible, and who know nothing of God's love in Jesus Christ. The thought of judgment as applied to them presents a perplexing problem. We cannot pretend to have an easy solution, but even such people are not entirely devoid of moral perception. The law is, as it were, written in their hearts so that they are not without liability. The responsibility of privilege will be a criterion of judgment. Jesus says that "unto whomsoever much is given, of him shall be much required". He warned the Jews who rejected Him, that the severity of their judgment would be in proportion to their opportunities. "It shall be more tolerable for Tyre and Sidon at the judgment, than for you", and again, "The men of Nineveh shall rise up in judgment with this generation and shall condemn it; because they repented at the preaching of Jonah, and behold, a greater than Jonah is here" (Luke 12. 48; 10. 14; Matt. 12. 41). We can only commend the heathen to God as unto a loving Creator, leaving, with meekness, their destiny to the Judge of all the earth, who will surely do right.

Lastly, there is that vast multitude of decent-living people who would be ashamed to fall below a certain standard of rectitude. Among them are those who make no profession of religion, though their behaviour often puts to shame those who do. The rest are associated with organised religion with varying degrees of sincerity and reality. The problem of judgment here is to us bewildering. Surely there must be some standard by which their complexity of achievement and failure can be resolved. The Bible gives an unmistakeable answer to this question. The standard is that of the perfect life of Jesus Christ. A formal profession of religion or even regular church-going cannot therefore be by themselves an insurance against condemnation. Jesus warns us that to build our hopes upon such a foundation is to build upon sand, with the certainty of disaster. He pictures those who in the judgment day will plead their religious devotion. "Have we not prophesied in thy name? and in thy name have cast out devils? and in thy name done many wonderful works?" But the answer comes, "I never knew you, depart from me" (Matt. 7. 21–27). Neither, we fear, will the non-churchgoer be justified because of the claim that he has done his best and cannot be expected to do more. If we are to be judged by the standard of righteousness which we have achieved, then the standard required is perfection. Archbishop William Temple once said, "It is not enough that we should be as good as people about us; nothing is enough except that we should be as good as God". That is, of course, impossible because all have sinned and come short of the glory of God, and therefore none of us can expect to escape judgment if we depend upon the record of our own deeds. Unless the sinner can be separated from his sin, he must inevitably be separated from God, who cannot dwell with sin.

God has provided a way by which this difficulty can be met. Jesus said He Himself was that "way".

Thus the first stage in judgment will be separation between those who have accepted God's way and those who are depending upon their own efforts. Our Lord used the metaphor of the Shepherd dividing his sheep from the goats. So, He said, will it be at the "end of the world"; the angels will "Sever the wicked from among the just". But who are the "wicked" and who are the "just"? We are told that at the judgment "another book was opened which is the book of life". It is called elsewhere the "Lamb's book of life". Jesus alluded to it when he told His disciples to rejoice because their names were written in heaven. St. Paul speaks of his fellow-labourers "whose names are written in the book of life" (Rev. 20. 12; 21. 27; Luke 10. 20; Phil. 4. 3). These will escape the judgment of condemnation, not because they are better than others, but because they have relied for their justification upon the perfect righteousness of Jesus. Nevertheless they must still appear before the Judgment Seat of Christ to give an account of their stewardship in His service. We cannot tell precisely what the outcome will be, but it may well include rewards for faithfulness.

In the consideration of the whole problem of judgment we may be perplexed to strike the proper balance between the goodness and the severity of God, but we may comfort ourselves with the certainty that the Judge of all the earth will do right, especially since He has given His own Son to die for our sins that we should not be condemned with the guilty. It is a fearful thing to fall into the hands of the living God, but over against the dark peril of condemnation is the shining promise that Jesus is able "to present you faultless before the presence of His glory with exceeding joy" (Jude 24).

6

What can we Know about Heaven?

WE cannot too often repeat that it is impossible for our finite minds to conceive the infinite. Two results follow from this limitation. First, God can describe for us what is infinite only in language that we can understand, which is bound to be inadequate; and secondly, we are not qualified to deny revealed truth which our limited spiritual perception is unable to comprehend. Moreover, our own thinking can be conditioned by the general climate of opinion, or by the lowered spiritual quality of the Church's life. We know that our national life reveals a much lower standard of appreciation of the things of the Spirit than it did, for example, during the Victorian era. This steady deterioration has inevitably affected us all, perhaps unconsciously. It has certainly affected the attitude of Christians to some of those articles of the faith which have been universally accepted for many centuries. The belief in the reality of heaven and hell was a very potent factor in moulding the character of the Englishman. It gave him a strong sense of accountability which determined his behaviour and earned for him a world-wide reputation for reliability. The Englishman's word was his bond. But gradually the idea of hell has receded into the background, partly because of a weakened sense of the reality of sin. The Church has largely ceased to speak about it, and this has inevitably resulted in doubts about, or even denial of, the reality of heaven. An inquiry instituted by the B.B.C. revealed an astonishing number of churchgoers who seemed to have no belief in a life after death. Our eyes have been turned away from the future to the present. We are no longer strangers and pilgrims on the earth; we are much more sensitive to the material things of this life and much less sensitive to, and interested in, the life to come. Yet we have not achieved peace of mind thereby, but rather a deep, unsatisfied hunger. Was it not because Dr. Billy Graham's preaching was so novel to this generation, that when he spoke fearlessly about heaven and hell, and about the inevitable choice to be made now, he attracted thousands of anxious people and aroused in many both a sense of danger and an eager anticipation to know more about the way to heaven?

WHAT IS HEAVEN LIKE?

Our Lord's references to heaven and "the kingdom of heaven" are far too numerous to record here; a glance at a concordance will show how long is the list. He advised the disciples to lay up treasure in heaven, and to rejoice because their names were written in heaven. He told them that He was going to prepare a place for them, and that there would be a reward for them there (Matt. 6. 20; Luke 10. 20; John 14. 2; Matt. 5. 12). When we search for a description of heaven we have again to remind ourselves that it is impossible for God to convey to us a precise impression of something which is beyond our comprehension. God is able to picture for us what we have never seen only by the use of such imagery as we can understand. Thus heaven is described as the New Jerusalem with streets of gold, gates of pearl, and foundations of precious stones, without need of the sun because its light never declines (Rev. 21). If such a place existed now on the earth, it would be regarded as one of the great wonders of the world, a place so fantastic that all would long to see it. But we may be sure that this description falls far short of the reality; it is the best that God can do in conveying to us a conception of the good things which pass man's understanding.

Most of us are not so concerned about the description of heaven as a place, as about the circumstances in which we shall live there. First and foremost is the fact that our Saviour will be there and we shall see Him face to face. To see in our Redeemer the marks of the nails, the evidence of His great love for us, will surely be a wonder to occupy eternity. There will be no more parting, no more tears, no more pain. The old things which make up this life and are never without their sad and imperfect side, will be done away; all things will be new (Rev. 21. 1–5).

WILL THERE BE RECOGNITION?

Shall we recognise our loved ones in heaven? It would be a shattering blow to the bereaved to be told that they would not. It would rob them of much of the consolation which the hope of the resurrection offers and deprive heaven of much of its joy. We have no specific guidance from Scripture, but the tenor of its teaching would seem to imply recognition. We have noted the promise that tears will be wiped away from off all faces. Is it not the bitterness of separation which caused those tears? Is it not meaningless to speak of "no more separation" if in fact we are not to be re-united? Ought not heaven to mean a renewal of communion but with a perfection we could never know in this life?

This will surely also be true of our relationship with the whole company of heaven. The quality of that fellowship will be on an altogether more exalted plane. The deep unity which is reserved in this life for blood-relations will embrace all the redeemed. That intimacy which can be enjoyed here only with caution and restraint because of our necessary conventions will be ours to the full. The human limitations which made it undesirable will have been removed. We need not fear a weakening of our existing family bonds because they are extended to include the whole household of God. Such a fear is caused by the imperfection of our human understanding. If we inquire too closely into every detail of an existence which is beyond all human conception, we shall be faced with insoluble and bewildering problems. We shall do well to be content with the broad presentation of Scripture that heaven will satisfy every perfect desire.

This principle should also guide us in answering the question "How shall we be occupied in heaven?" We may be sure that those who have spent their lives in God's service on earth will continue to serve Him in the new life, but without the limitations and defects which hindered them here.

A twofold activity is indicated in the Bible: worship and service. We smile at our forebears, who thought of heaven in terms of golden harps strung and tuned for endless years, but such glimpses as we are permitted into the heavenly sphere reveal the whole company of heaven at worship. Isaiah saw the Lord high and lifted up and heard the song "Holy, holy, holy is the Lord of Hosts". In Revelation, chapter 7, we see a vision of the redeemed standing before the throne in adoring worship.

They are also described as serving Him day and night in His temple. What this service may be we cannot tell, but we may find a clue in the parable of the Pounds in which the master who returned from a long absence to call his servants to account, gave them increased responsibility in proportion to their faithfulness (Luke 19). We may assume that our talents will be given back to us for further use unlimited by human frailty. Our service in eternity will be related to our fidelity in time.

THE COMMUNITY OF HEAVEN

We shall not be alone in our rapture. Heaven will be a community. The Church of God will be there, those who have "washed their robes and made them white in the blood of the Lamb". The nations of them that are saved will walk in it; even the kings of the earth will bring their glory and honour into it, casting down their crowns before Him who sits on the throne (Rev. 21). Together we shall serve Him. The tensions and strains which now affect personal relationships, and cause so much mental and physical illness, will give way to poise and harmonious accord. The inevitable diversities of opinion on spiritual matters which so sadly divide Christians will be resolved in a unity of complete understanding. The perfect life, free from frustration, for which we long, and which we sorrowfully admit can never be ours on earth, will become a reality in heaven. All this because Jesus has redeemed us by His own death. In that better land we shall know fully what we owe to Him.

Heaven, then, will be to live with God forever. But we must admit that this definition will embarrass rather than attract some people. They would view with alarm the thought of such close contact with the Deity. This brings into sharp relief the broken relationship between God and man, and the gulf which must be bridged if man is to dwell with God—and enjoy it. It is obvious that a radical change in his nature is needed, something far more fundamental than reformation or improvement. He must be not just a better man but a new man, and that seems impossible. And yet it is not impossible, for every day the experience comes to some by which their relationship to God is transformed; it is the experience which Jesus called being "born again". We become a new creation in Christ Jesus. Instead of thinking of God as a remote and fearsome Deity, we find that we are partakers of the Divine Nature; we are adopted into the family of God; God becomes to us our "Father" (Rom. 8. 14–15). This happy relationship grows and deepens. We become conscious of our pilgrim status. Death is no longer the terminus of our journey, but the threshold of our heavenly home where our Father and the family wait to welcome us to abide in His presence for ever.

—7—

What must we Do to enter Heaven?

WE have tried, thus far, to show what the Bible says and what our Church believes about the future life, and we have seen that for those who are "in Christ" there is a blessed hope and assurance that they will be "for ever with the Lord". We have, in passing, said something about the conditions which make this possible for us. But it may be that you are not clear about this and are still asking the question, "What have we to do to be sure of eternal life?" Let me try to answer this question as simply as possible, taking the Bible as our guide and confirming our conclusions, if we can, by comparing them with the conclusions of other Christians as seen in the formularies of our Church.

We must start from the truth that God is a holy God; that is to say we have to add to His power, majesty and wisdom, His moral perfection. He is absolutely pure and free from all taint of sin. Sin cannot exist in His presence. "Thou art of purer eyes than to behold evil, and canst not look on iniquity." In Isaiah's vision of the Lord in the Temple the seraphim cried one to another "Holy, holy, holy, is the Lord of Hosts" (Isa. 6. 3). The scriptural method of emphasising superlative quality is repetition. When Isaiah would stress the perfection of God's peace he says, "Thou wilt keep him in perfect peace whose mind is stayed on thee" (26. 3), but the original is not "perfect peace" but "peace, peace". In Isaiah 6, however, the word "holy" is repeated three times to indicate that the holiness of God is something exceeding all our superlatives. So in our

49

Service of Holy Communion we unite in praising God with the same words, "Holy, holy, holy, Lord God of Hosts, heaven and earth are full of Thy glory".

As it is impossible to understand fully the holiness of God, so it is equally impossible for us fully to realise the measure of our sinfulness. We are all sinners. "There is none righteous, no, not one." All have sinned, and fall short of God's holiness. Let us be clear about this. It is not how often we have sinned, or whether we have been guilty of great crimes or conventional sins; it is rather that we are sinners because we have a sinful nature. We naturally measure ourselves by the standard of other people—in two ways. We say we are not like those who steal, or commit crimes of violence, or live immoral lives; and we also say, "I am as good as my neighbour. I live an honest life and do my best." The important fact is not that we have sinned great or little sins, but that we have *sinned*, that we often find it easier to do what is wrong than what is right, that we have a natural bias towards wrong which we must constantly resist. The Psalmist says, "Behold, I was shapen in iniquity, and in sin did my mother conceive me", and Isaiah declares that even our "righteousnesses are as filthy rags" (Ps. 51. 5; Isa. 64. 6).

SIN SEPARATES US FROM GOD

If it is hard for us to understand the true extent of our sinfulness, it is still harder to understand the vast gulf which exists between our sinfulness and God's holiness. The stars look bright and clear against the dark background of the night sky, but when the sun arises in all its glory, their brilliance fades and disappears. So against the dark background of evil in the world to-day, the lives of good people seem to shine brightly, but in the blinding light of the Sun of righteousness their goodness vanishes and is lost.

It is our sin which separates us from God and makes it impossible for us to dwell with Him in heaven. "Your iniquities have separated between you and your God" (Isa. 59. 2).

Man's position, therefore, apart from God, is seen to be hopeless. There is nothing he can do, or achieve, which will put right the fundamental hindrance to his acceptance with God. No amount of good works will suffice, for we can never reach God's standard of goodness. We may be regular churchgoers, we may even be office-bearers in the Church, but this will not be enough. The Lord Jesus warned the religious people of His day against the danger of rejecting God's provision for their salvation and presuming to think that their own would be sufficient. In the story of the wedding feast (Matt. 22. 13) one guest insisted upon coming in his own clothes, in spite of the fact that the condition of the invitation was that suitable dress would be provided; and he was cast out. We may think that our own righteousness is sufficient to gain an entrance to heaven, but the condition is that we are clothed in the righteousness which God provides. The rich young ruler asked our Lord what he must *do* to inherit eternal life. Jesus referred him to the law; and he replied that he had kept it; what else must he do? But the Lord was quickly able to disabuse him of the idea that he had reached God's standard, and he went away sorrowful (Luke 18. 18 f.). The disciples, who were listening, were astonished, and exclaimed, "Who then can be saved?" Our Lord replied, in effect, that no one could be saved by attempting to achieve a sufficient standard of goodness, but "the things that are impossible with men are possible with God".

What are we to do then? We may even be prepared to die for our sins, but that is just what God does not want us to do. He wants us to live, and to live with Him; and because He is a God of love, as well as a holy God,

He has in fact, in the person of His Son, died instead of us that we might live. This is the "good news", the "Gospel", that in spite of the apparent hopelessness of our position, God has provided a way whereby our sins can be forgiven and we can be made fit to dwell with Him. That way is Jesus Christ. There is no other way. We are often told that there are many roads to heaven, but that is not the verdict of Scripture. There are many roads to Jesus Christ, but we must come first to Him. John Bunyan, in the *Pilgrim's Progress*, made every pilgrim enter by the "wicket gate". There was no other way, and there is no other name under heaven beside that of Jesus Christ whereby we may reach the goal of God's presence (Acts 4. 12).

CHRIST DIED FOR OUR SINS

It is the death of Christ which makes it possible. Of course His birth, His life, His resurrection, and His ascension were all part of God's plan, but the Cross is central. His death was not just the inevitable end of His earthly life. To the disciples it was an overwhelming and inexplicable disaster. After His resurrection Jesus walked with two of them from Jerusalem to Emmaus. As they walked He showed them how the Old Testament foretold His coming and its purpose, that He should die for the sins of the world (Luke 24. 25–27). He repeated this to all the disciples later, and this Good News transformed them from disillusioned men into the triumphant and confident people who "turned the world upside down".

Christ died for our sins. That is the simplest way to express the Gospel; but within this formula is such a wealth of meaning that the resources of language would be exhausted to describe it. St. Peter, in his first epistle (3. 18), says, "Christ also once suffered for sins, the just for the unjust, that He might bring us to God".

There is a three-fold statement here. First, that *Christ died for our sins*. In some mysterious way which it is beyond our ability to understand, our Saviour "bore our sins" on the Cross. St. Paul goes so far as to say "he was made to be sin for us". Secondly, He, the just One, did this *on behalf of the unjust* ones; the perfect for the imperfect. He alone could do that because He had no sins of His own. "There was no other good enough to pay the price of sin." Thirdly, He did this *to bring us to God*. Sin makes it impossible for us to approach God. He, by removing sin, is able to introduce us into His presence. We are alienated from God like the prodigal in the far country: He brings us back into the Father's home. Notice that He did this "once". His death was not incidental like the undeserved sufferings of the Christians to whom Peter was writing. It was purposeful: it was determined. It was once for all, never to be repeated, never again to be needed, because it had achieved the desired end—our welcome into the family of God on earth and our access into the presence of God in heaven.

WHAT MUST WE DO?

What, then, have we to do? First, we must acknowledge our sins and confess our unworthiness, turning to God in true repentance. We must come to the point where we admit that we can make no contribution ourselves to achieve that justification in the sight of God of which we have spoken, but that it is only possible by faith in what Jesus Christ has done for us. Article XI puts it thus: "We are accounted righteous before God, only for the merit of our Lord and Saviour Jesus Christ by faith, and not for our own works or deservings." This statement is based upon the teaching of the Bible. Romans, chapter 3, declares that we are "justified freely by his grace through the redemption that is in Christ

Jesus". We can work to earn the wages of sin, but
eternal life is a free gift. We cannot deserve it; we can
only accept it. Even the faith by which we accept it is
not our own; it is the gift of God (Eph. 2. 8). Therefore
none of us can boast before God or before one another.
We are all alike equally dependent upon the grace and
mercy of God.

Next, we must do what St. Paul advised the Philip-
pian gaoler to do when he asked the same question,
namely, believe on the Lord Jesus Christ. But at this
point there must be a word of caution. Beware of thinking that "believing" means merely an intellectual assent
to a number of propositions about Jesus Christ. It
means much more than this. It involves also the logical
implication of acting upon that admission. Let me try
to explain. If you were to protest vehemently your confidence in the safety of air travel, and yet refused in any
circumstances to board an aircraft, your protestations
would not carry conviction. If we say we believe that
Jesus obtained forgiveness of our sins by His death on
the Cross, then we must live as those who have accepted
His forgiveness. We must acknowledge Him as our
Saviour and submit ourselves to His lordship, boldly
claiming that what He has promised He is able also to
perform.

If I take this step, how can I be sure that it is true and
that I have in fact passed from death unto life? The
answer is found in the Christian doctrine of assurance.
Perhaps there is no other doctrine which is so heavily
underscored in Scripture as this. There are so many
unequivocal guarantees, that it would be quite impossible to quote even a small proportion of them here.
What could be clearer than these words of our Saviour:
"Verily, verily, I say unto you, he that heareth my
word, and believeth on Him that sent me, hath everlasting life, and shall not come into condemnation; but
is passed from death unto life" (John 5. 24)? Words

could hardly make more plain that everlasting life is a present possession, and that neither death nor judgment can rob us of it. Here, then, is God's guarantee; but we can only be convinced as we take Him at His word.

"As many as received him, to them gave he power to become the sons of God, even to them that believe on his name" (John 1. 12). When we receive Him, we are born into God's family and God becomes our Father; our relationship to Him and His whole family has been revolutionised. This is *one way* by which we know that our act of acceptance of His offer has really made a change in us. *Another* is that He gives us an inward confidence of the new life of Christ which is ours, *and finally* we find ourselves with a new love for our fellow-Christians: "We know that we have passed from death unto life, because we love the brethren" (1 John 3. 14).

For the Christian, then, death is not a calamity, a leap in the dark, or just the end of a happy life. It is the gateway into a fuller and more wonderful experience. We have seen how God has looked upon our sad estate, made it possible for us to enter into life, and given us the assurance of dwelling with Him hereafter. But we have also seen that this happy outcome will not take place in the natural course of events; it depends upon our receiving by an act of decision what God offers to us. Let us beware of missing this gift through failure on our part to do what is necessary to secure so great a prize.

III

PRACTICAL APPLICATIONS

The Burial Service

THE Burial Service in the Book of Common Prayer is unfamiliar to most people because they hear it infrequently. For this reason they do not readily understand it or derive that consolation from it which it ought to give.

I suggest that we look at it together. It will help if you have your Prayer Book (a borrowed one, if necessary) open before you. The service will be found among those beginning with the Baptism of Infants which follow the Holy Communion.

THE SERVICE IN CHURCH

Let us imagine ourselves sitting in church awaiting the arrival of the cortège. Its entrance is heralded by the recital of some sentences from the Bible, the first of which is "I am the resurrection and the life, saith the Lord: he that believeth in me, though he were dead, yet shall he live: and whosoever liveth and believeth in me shall never die". We are reminded that if Christ is our life now, He will be our resurrection in the last day.

As the procession continues on its way, we hear the second sentence, which Handel has set to such lovely music in his *Messiah*—"I know that my redeemer liveth", and though my body may die and decay "yet in my flesh shall I see God; whom I shall see for myself, and mine eyes shall behold, and not another". Here we assert our faith in the resurrection of the body; we shall see our Redeemer face to face. There follows the third sentence, the first part of which is "We brought nothing into this world, and it is certain we can carry nothing out", and the second part is the word of Job after he had lost his family and his possessions, "The Lord gave, and the Lord hath taken away; blessed be the name of the Lord." We acknowledge that what God has taken from us, He first gave us, and therefore all He does is well.

Sometimes other sentences may be added until those in the procession have reached their places and the service proper is ready to begin. We are now able to approach this sad occasion in the right spirit. Sorrow, of course, there must be, but it is relieved by the knowledge that our loss is only temporary; we look forward to the day of resurrection and reunion.

A psalm is now sung. If we were to choose what we should sing, it might not be either of those found in the Prayer Book. They dwell, a little more than we like, upon the brevity of life and the inevitability of death. We may therefore find that the 23rd Psalm is used instead, the exquisite Shepherd Psalm, which has become so popular in its paraphrase set to the tune *Crimond*.

After the psalm a passage of Scripture is read. It is usually part of the wonderful 15th chapter of 1 Corinthians. In an earlier chapter we saw that Paul here not only declares the *fact* of the resurrection, but tells us something about the *character* of the resurrection body as well. Though it will retain some relation to the present body, it will be a new creation invested with glorious powers. Because of its length, this chapter is often either shortened or replaced by some alternative reading. This may be 2 Corinthians 4. 8–18, which exhorts us not to dwell too much upon our sorrow but to look away to the things eternal; or 2 Corinthians 5. 5–10, which reminds us that our earthly body is only a temporary home; or 1 Thessalonians 4. 13–18, which speaks of the return of the Lord Jesus and our reunion with our loved ones at the resurrection; or Revelation 7. 9–17 or 21. 1–7, both describing the blissful state of the redeemed in heaven. Thus far everything has been in the words of Scripture, but now a hymn may be sung and an address may be given.

When our service was compiled, most churches were surrounded by churchyards in which the burial took place. The service might therefore be entirely at the graveside or, up to the point that we have now reached, in church. At this stage everyone would proceed to the grave for the remainder of the prayers. But to-day, when the grave may be some distance from the church, as much of the service as possible is read in the church or in the cemetery chapel, and only the brief prayers of committal at the grave. If, on the other hand, the body is to be cremated, the whole service will probably take place in the chapel of the crematorium.

We will assume that our service continues in church. After the address there may be another hymn, and this part concludes with prayers. The first thanks God for the assurance that our loved one is "in joy and felicity, far from the miseries of this sinful world", and asks that the time may soon come when we too "may have our perfect consummation and bliss" in God's everlasting glory. Here is the prayer in full:

Almighty God, with whom do live the spirits of them that depart hence in the Lord, and with whom the souls of the faithful, after they are delivered from the burden of the flesh, are in joy and felicity; we give Thee hearty thanks for that it hath pleased thee to deliver this our *brother* [or *sister*] out of the miseries of this sinful world; beseeching thee, that it may please thee, of thy gracious goodness, shortly to accomplish the number of Thine elect, and to hasten thy Kingdom; that we, with all those that are departed in the true faith of thy holy Name, may have our perfect consummation and bliss, both in body and soul, in thy eternal and everlasting glory; through Jesus Christ our Lord. Amen.

The second prayer is a Collect which recites the Scriptural promises of resurrection and requests that when our turn comes to die we too may rest in Jesus and be found acceptable in His sight:

O merciful God, the Father of our Lord Jesus Christ, who is the Resurrection and the Life; in whom whosoever believeth shall live, though he die; and whosoever liveth, and believeth in him, shall not die eternally; who also hath taught us (by his holy Apostle Saint Paul) not to be sorry, as men without hope, for them that sleep in him; we meekly beseech thee, O Father, to raise us from the death of sin unto the life of righteousness; that, when we shall depart this life, we may rest in him, as our hope is this our *brother* [or *sister*] doth; and that, at the general resurrection in the last day, we may be found acceptable in Thy sight; and receive that blessing, which Thy well-beloved Son shall then pronounce to all that love and fear Thee, saying, Come, ye blessed children of my Father, receive the kingdom prepared for you from the beginning of the world; Grant this, we beseech thee, O merciful Father, through Jesus Christ, our Mediator and Redeemer. Amen.

It is customary to add here a prayer for those who mourn.

THE COMMITTAL

The coffin is now taken from the church to the grave. While preparations are being made to lower it into its last resting place, we go back to that part of the service which was omitted in church. The minister reads some sentences which bring home to us the fleeting character of life and close with an appeal to our merciful Saviour to deliver us from the punishment of our sins. As an alternative to these words a portion of Psalm 103 is sometimes read; it assures us of the mercy of the Lord, which is timeless and eternal.

As the coffin is lowered into the grave (or slowly vanishes from sight in the crematorium chapel), the gracious prayer of committal is spoken, acknowledging that the soul of the departed loved one has gone to be with the Lord Himself and that we commit the body to the earth (or the fire) "in sure and certain hope of the resurrection to eternal life", knowing that the poor mortal body will be made "like unto His glorious body".

Now the words of Revelation 14. 13 ring out: "I heard a voice from heaven, saying unto me, write, From henceforth blessed are the dead which die in the Lord." Happy dead! For them there is no more separation. They lived in Him, died in Him, and are now with Him. As we take farewell until the day dawns and the shadows flee away, it is not with undiluted sorrow, for we leave them in bliss, though we must now face the world without them. Our thoughts turn to ourselves as we break into the words "Lord have mercy upon us", and then join in the Lord's Prayer. The Grace or the blessing follows; the service is over, and we depart.

You may have noticed three characteristics of this Prayer Book Service. The first is its close accord with both the words and the teaching of the Bible, thus giving us a conviction of authority for the message of hope which permeates the whole.

The second is that it faces the hard and unpleasant facts of the situation. We may feel that it dwells unnecessarily upon the sombre side of death and is therefore out of tune with our rather sensitive age. In our sympathy for the feelings of the bereaved we sometimes

E

substitute words (but still the words of Scripture) of a deeper tenderness and more cheerful hopefulness, where it appears necessary. Some will question the wisdom of these changes, but they are very common to-day.

The third characteristic is the note of confidence concerning the future, which is heard on every page. Though we may return from the ordeal of the funeral service with a consciousness of loneliness, yet we must have been warmed by the nearness of the Lord and by the love He bestows, and our sorrow will have been lightened by the bright prospect of the resurrection morning.

— 9 —

How to be Brave in Bereavement

"WHAT I do thou knowest not now; but thou shalt know hereafter" (John 13. 7). Jesus spoke these words to the embarrassed disciples when He washed their feet. They are equally applicable to the mystery of suffering to-day. There must be few adults who have not known the bitterness of bereavement, with perhaps a sense of complete helplessness in the face of sorrow. We can, therefore, have a deep fellow-feeling with those who are passing through this sad experience. What can I say to comfort you?

First of all, remember that time is a great healer. Sir Winston Churchill once said, "Only faith in a life after death, in a brighter world where dear ones meet again —only that, and the measured tramp of time, can give consolation". It may be hard to believe that we can ever be able to enjoy life again, or adapt ourselves to a situation from which all the joy seems to have been taken. But we have only to recall our experiences during the War to be convinced of the amazing ability of the human spirit to adjust itself to conditions which, in cold thought, would seem unbearable.

There will be a great temptation to indulge in morbid self-pity, but this temptation should be resisted at all costs. Self-pity tends to alienate sympathy rather than to attract it. There will be a wealth of loving understanding from friends and neighbours, and the courage with which we bear our sorrow will be a help to them and, of course, a blessing to ourselves.

It is wise to keep busy. At the time of bereavement

there is so much to be done that our minds are mercifully occupied, but when the immediate tasks have been completed and the funeral is over, we have more time to brood over our changed circumstances, and we begin to realise just what they are going to mean. This is the dangerous time, and it is more than ever essential, if we are not already occupied, to see that time does not hang heavily on our hands. Nothing is so beneficial at such a time as helping other people; turning our thoughts away from our own sorrows to those of others. We are not alone in our grief; there are many passing along the same road whose circumstances may be even worse than our own; and perhaps some of them, unlike ourselves, have no knowledge of the Lord Jesus and the assurance which He gives. For them, bereavement must indeed be a bleak and dreadful thing; what an opportunity for us to share with them that confidence in God's love which gives us hope!

It is, of course, this sure and certain hope which will be your great comfort at such a time. But perhaps you are finding, as some do, that your senses are numbed by the blow which you have received, and that the poignancy of your suffering is greater than the consolation which you should gain from the faith you hold. It may even be that you are troubled and distressed because the faith which you have always enjoyed about the "life after death in a brighter world where dear ones meet again" has failed you just when you needed it most. Do not let this trouble you overmuch. It is only a passing effect of your bereavement. We may have had the experience in physical illness when we thought that we had lost our health altogether and would never be well again; but recovery has followed and we have realised that our loss of confidence was a passing result of physical weakness. So it is in the mental strain through which you are passing; it has its physical effects which we must recognise as temporary, and incidentally as an occasion which the Evil One is not slow to use to weaken our trust in the Lord Jesus.

THE LOVE OF GOD

How are we to meet this Impostor? First, I would suggest, by remembering God's love for us. It was so great that He was willing to give His Son to die upon the Cross to secure our eternal nearness to Himself. What better proof could we ask? If you find it very difficult to understand why, if God loves you, He has allowed this calamity to fall upon you, will you think of Calvary? There is so much that we cannot understand. There was so much that even the disciples did not understand until the Resurrection had enlightened them. But we do know that "it was for us He hung and suffered there". Therefore it is reasonable to trust His love even though we cannot comprehend His providence. Job, whose sufferings were beyond anything we could be called upon to endure, said, "He knoweth the way that I take: when He hath tried me, I shall come forth as gold" (Job 23. 10). Trust Him even if you cannot understand.

God has given us a memorial of His love for us in the Lord's Supper instituted on the night of His betrayal. He intended it to be a perpetual remembrance of "the exceeding great love of our Master, and only Saviour, Jesus Christ, thus dying for us, and the innumerable benefits which by His precious blood-shedding He hath obtained to us". As we draw near and take the symbols of our redemption, the bread broken and the wine poured out, we acknowledge His infinite care for us and His lordship over our lives. In this supreme act of thanksgiving we declare our faith in a love so universal that it embraces the sin and sorrow of the whole human race, and yet so personal that our own deep sorrow is His intimate concern. He who bore the darkness of separation upon the Cross draws near to us in tender sympathy and "assures us thereby of His favour and goodness towards us".

These tokens of His love also provide that spiritual food which strengthens us to bear the burdens which are laid upon us, and nourishes our souls that we may be able to endure manfully unto the end. They assure us also that we are incorporated into that blessed company of faithful people we call the "Church". We are members of the body of Christ, and in that holy fellowship we shall find our sorrow shared and relieved. Thus, as our intimacy with our Saviour deepens into union with Him, we shall learn to trust when we cannot see.

Handley Moule, a former saintly Bishop of Durham, used to tell the story of an old book-marker which he treasured because it belonged to his mother. It was a card pierced with holes, and a text was worked on it in blue silk. One side of the card showed a tangle of confused and crossing threads, but on the other side in beautifully clear letters, *produced by the tangled stitches*, were the words GOD IS LOVE. From this he drew a parable that here on earth we are, as it were, looking at the "wrong side" of God's work upon our lives. It seems so meaningless and difficult to understand, but one day we shall see the "other side" and wonder at the loving purposes of God. Bishop Moule went on to tell the following story of this book-marker. "Seven years ago, February 21, 1909, I took that dear book-marker up into a pulpit, and let it preach a sermon to stricken hearts. At West Stanley, in County Durham, an awful pit disaster had occurred; one hundred and sixty-nine men and lads had died together of that explosion. On the Sunday evening following I preached there, to a church quite full of mourners. I held up my mother's card to them, and pointed out its message of faith and hope. And I happen to know that the old book-marker brought more light and help to the mourners that night than all the rest of my sermon put together."[1] Trust Him, even if you cannot understand. William Cowper, the great hymn writer, has put into words just what we need to know to-day.

> "His purposes will ripen fast,
>   Unfolding every hour:
> The bud may have a bitter taste,
>   But sweet will be the flower.

> "Blind unbelief is sure to err,
>   And scan His work in vain;
> God is His own interpreter,
>   And He will make it plain."

THE FRIENDSHIP OF JESUS

Next I would counsel you in the loneliness of your bereavement to discover for yourself the friendship and the sympathy of the Lord Jesus. The disciples were ordinary people like ourselves, and they must have realised how far removed from them He was in His goodness and power, and yet He called them His friends. "I call you not servants . . . but I have called you friends" (John 15. 15). His friendship for us is equally certain because His love is the same.

The story of His human life is the story of His sympathy shown to those in sorrow, and sickness, and need. No one ever appealed to Him in vain. There were times when the disciples discouraged those who approached Him, but Jesus rebuked them and responded to the plea of the sick and suffering. There are two occasions where we read that Jesus wept, and it is significant that one of them was concerned with a bereavement. Do not therefore ignore His thought for

---

[1] *Christ and Sorrow*, H. C. G. Moule, p. 66.

you, but cast "all your care upon Him; for He careth for you" (1 Pet. 5. 7).

It is not only His friendship and sympathy which He gives us; we have the promise of His presence too. "Lo, I am with you all the days", said the Lord Jesus (Matt. 28. 20). When He was about to leave His disciples, He explained to them that this would be to their advantage, for so long as His physical presence remained, He could not be in more than one place at a time. In a mysterious way, which is beyond explanation, He is closer to us now than if He were still with us in the flesh. Cultivate His companionship and you will find infinite solace, and courage more than human.

THE FELLOWSHIP OF CHRISTIANS

Thirdly, do not underestimate the value of fellowship and worship within the Church, "the household of God". St. Paul thinks of the Christian family in terms which are more intimate than that of an earthly family. He speaks of it as one body, with Christ as the Head. "If one member suffers", says St. Paul, "all the members suffer with it" (1 Cor. 13. 26). There is a deep and loving spiritual affinity between the members of Christ's body. Within this circle you will find a bond of fellow-feeling which will give you courage to bear your sorrow.

This fellowship will be found with individual Christians, but it can only be fulfilled in the larger community of the Church. There you will also discover the additional help which comes through corporate worship. The regular meeting with others Sunday by Sunday will be a source of inspiration. You will gain from the services themselves comfort and strength: the hymns will speak to you with a new meaning; the reading of the lessons will seem as if they were meant for you alone;

the prayers will be for you too, and you will know that many of those present will have you and your need in their thoughts and prayers. The sermon will bring you new thoughts of God's love and care, and provide new ways of meeting your trial triumphantly. Worship can lift us out of ourselves. Even when we find it hard to pray, the prayers and praises of the congregation can bear us up into the presence of God.

This does not exhaust the blessings which the fellowship of other Christians can give. I would urge you to throw yourself into the activities of the Church during the week. Be an *active* member. There is so much that you can do, and it will help to keep you from dwelling too much upon your sorrow. In the mid-week Bible Study circle, in the prayer meeting, in the Women's Fellowship or the Men's Club, in active service such as visiting; in all these ways and in many others you will find, not only blessing for yourself, but the opportunity of helping to cheer others.

PRAYER AND BIBLE READING

There is another means of grace which will help you n your bereavement. It is the exercise of Prayer and Bible Study. The Bible is God's word to man. We may, therefore, confidently expect to find that it will speak to our special need. We saw how the two disciples on the Emmaus road were plunged in dark despair by the bereavement which they suffered through the death of their Master, and how He consoled them, not as we should expect, by revealing Himself to them as risen again, but by turning their thoughts to the word of God. "He expounded unto them in all the Scriptures the things concerning Himself." When, at last, they realised with a thrill of joy that it was the Master Himself, they confessed that He had already lifted them out of their despair by the exposition of God's Holy Word. "Did not our heart burn within us, while He talked with us by the way?" (Luke 24. 27 and 32). And the same Lord Jesus will talk to you and open to you the consolations of His word if you seek Him there. Read your Bible every day. You will find it helpful to link up with an organisation which provides a scheme of daily readings with explanatory notes. Thus, with thousands of other readers, you will feed on the Bread of Life to the nourishment of your soul.

In a close and intimate friendship there must always be, as it were, a two-way traffic. Communication is never all on one side. Prayer and Bible reading should go together, and prayer is one of the ways in which God has provided for our comfort and guidance. Prayer is companionship with God, and, how much you need that companionship now! In its rich enjoyment you can find a balm for your wounded spirit. He will come very close to you; and His nearness is never more sure than when we are so overwhelmed with grief that we cannot frame words to express it.

But the privilege of prayer calls for perseverance. Nothing that is worth-while is easy. The most important thing, and quite the most difficult, is to be conscious of His nearness. It is so easy to slip into a habit of careless prayer; praying for this and that without any thought of the great unseen Listener. God uses our trials to bless us, for in sorrow prayer cannot be formal or thoughtless. It is directed to One from whom we long for help, and it is only as we are sure of His attention that we can pray with any hope.

And we *can* be sure of a sympathetic reception, "for we have not an high priest which cannot be touched with the feeling of our infirmities; but was in all points tempted like as we are, yet without sin. Let us therefore come boldly unto the throne of grace, that we may obtain mercy, and find grace to help in time of need"

(Heb. 4. 15–16). If we need a convincing guarantee of this, we find it in St. Paul's words "He that spared not His own Son, but delivered Him up for us all, how shall He not with Him also freely give us all things?" (Rom. 8. 32).

Do not be too troubled about the use of words. God knows our inmost hearts, and when we are so overwhelmed that we cannot find words to speak, we can, as it were, look up to Him in mute appeal. Archbishop Davidson said, "As one grows older I find that meditation takes the place of more definite prayer and that one thinks upon people and problems and work as in the presence of God".

We should beware of formality or of being bound by conventional ideas about prayer. A great saint who wrote early in this century said, "Many would probably spend a much longer time in communion with our Lord than they do, if they could bring themselves to believe that standing, walking, sitting, and even lying down may be attitudes of prayer". Bishop Moule of Durham said, "recollectedness and concentration of heart and mind are usually quickened in my case by a reverent standing attitude . . . or by walking up and down, either indoors or, as I love to do when possible, in the open air. A garden may prove a very hallowed oratory". Each of us must find the way which in his case is most conducive to concentration, forgetfulness of self, and consciousness of the presence of the Lord.

These times of secret prayer in the presence of the Master will be very precious. But let us not forget, too, that corporate prayer with others can also bring relief. It may be with a dear friend, or with a group of people, or in church with the great congregation.

It is hard to be brave when we lose our nearest and dearest, but through the love and compassion of God in

Christ we shall find courage and strength to endure, and we shall discover that

> "There is no death! What seems so is transition.
> This life of mortal breath
> Is but a suburb of the life Elysian,
> Whose portal we call Death."

Preparing for Death

THERE is a story told of Lord Cecil, Bishop of Exeter, who was notorious for his absent-mindedness. Travelling by train one day, the inspector came to examine tickets. The Bishop could not find his. After much searching, the inspector, who knew the Bishop well, said, "Never mind, my lord, don't worry, it doesn't matter". "Oh, but it does matter," said the Bishop, "how am I to know where I am going?"

We laugh at the Bishop and think it rather ridiculous, but do we know where *we* are going at the end of life's journey? Unless Jesus Christ comes again in our lifetime, every one of us must face the certainty of death. Either event may come unexpectedly and find us unprepared. Most people put off this vital consideration either because it is too uncomfortable to think about, or because (they say), "We don't know anything about the future; so why worry?"; or because they decide it is time enough to think about it when they get nearer to the end—"Life is too short to spend time worrying about the future!" Of course none of these excuses is really valid. This life is so short in relation to eternity that it would be almost impossible to conceive a comparable measurement. The time is therefore relatively very limited in which to make our dispositions for eternity, yet the importance of ensuring the proper enjoyment of our endless future is beyond all calculation. The expectation of life has increased in our own day, so that we may feel justified in the natural course of events to defer a decision about our future, but the incidence of sudden death appears to be on the increase, so that we cannot be certain of time to put our house in order.

We have dwelt at some length in Chapter 7 upon the way by which we may come to God through Jesus Christ and receive forgiveness of sin, enter at once upon that eternal life which is uninterrupted by death, and thus ensure that as we live in Christ here we shall dwell with Christ hereafter. It involves a decision which in turn determines our destiny. The crisis may be thrust upon us when we least expect it. Therefore the first essential in preparing for death is to heed our Lord's urgent injunction, "Be ye therefore ready" (Luke 12. 40).

THE TIME TO PREPARE

You will already have guessed that, in spite of its title, this chapter is not meant only for those who are nearing the gates of death. The time to prepare for death is *now*, and the younger we are the better. It is a curious psychological paradox that the age-group most ready and willing to face this challenge is the teen-age group. It may be because life for them has always been made up of change (from infancy to childhood and adolescence) that they have not had time to settle into the rut from which it is difficult to prise out the middle-aged. Also they are on the threshold of life with all its hopes and possibilities, and they are ready to face it wholly and face it squarely. Thus many young people enter into newness of life at an early age, and their whole life is transformed by the power and friendship of Jesus Christ and freed from fear and anxiety about the future. The truth is that the older we become, the more diffi-cult it is to make decisions. It is therefore never too early to prepare for death.

If as Christians our faith in all that the Bible teaches about the next life is sincere, we ought to look forward to death as did St. Paul. The title of this chapter could then be "How to Enjoy Heaven Here and Now". We should be living in the light of eternity, always conscious of our pilgrim status. As strangers and foreigners upon the earth, we adjust ourselves to our temporary home, but our hearts are in our homeland and we long for our exile to end. Our goal is the City of God, where we join "the spirits of just men made perfect, the general assembly and Church of the firstborn, an innumerable company of angels, Jesus the mediator of the new covenant, and God the Judge of all" (Heb. 12. 22–24).

We would do well to try to recover in our generation that awareness of the spiritual realm which was a mark of our fathers, both ancient and modern. The extent to which they lived in the happy consciousness of their heavenly citizenship is reflected in the remarkable number of hymns which carry their thoughts away to that blissful land. Unlike the Hebrew exiles by the waters of Babylon, who said, "How shall we sing the Lord's song in a strange land?" they, like most exiles, were never tired of the songs of their homeland. Many of these songs have fallen into disuse and are unknown to us, but most of us will know "For ever with the Lord" and "For thee O dear, dear country". That exquisite hymn "There is a land of pure delight" must have thrilled all of us, and perhaps, too, "There is a blessed home". Though we rather despise them, "Jerusalem the golden" and "Jerusalem my happy home" have brought joy to countless spirits. We would do well to read and ponder these hymns, in conjunction with the passages of the Bible upon which they are based.

It was not only the saints among our forebears who lived in the light of eternity. This beneficial outlook influenced the whole nation. R. C. K. Ensor, in his *England 1870–1914*, says this other-wordliness was an everyday conviction and induced "a highly civilised people to put pleasure in the background, and what it conceived to be duty in the foreground, to a quite exceptional degree" (p. 138). It is not difficult to conceive how a recovery of this attitude would transform our present discontents! It would also wean us away from our preoccupation with the things of this life.

We are so immersed in things temporal, and so much of our time and thought is given to the improvement of our standard of living; there are so many new inventions to offer us opportunities for undreamed-of delights, and so much to make life here a fascinating adventure, that it is little wonder we give less and less thought to the things eternal. We must sedulously guard against this danger, and we can do so only by turning our minds constantly away from this world to the next. It is fatally easy to get "bedded-down" in our environment until, like Lot in the Old Testament story, we have to be rescued by force from the peril of a false security.

It is obvious that we must cultivate a familiarity with the heavenly kingdom. As we persevere in doing so, it will become second nature to us. We must "practise the presence of Christ". The "morning watch" will set the tone for the whole day, but we should learn to achieve the attitude in which we continually and spontaneously turn to the Lord Jesus in unspoken prayer about every concern of our daily lives. Living thus in the conscious companionship of the Lord is the most practical preparation for living forever with Him. Death will then be not even an interruption of that blessed experience, but merely the signal for the end of its imperfect enjoyment and the beginning of its perfect fulfilment. A lively expectation of the Lord's return would also ensure that we were "in the Spirit" when the day of the Lord dawned.

PUTTING OUR HOUSE IN ORDER

Something must be said of the more mundane and yet very practical side of preparation for death. This applies especially to those who are married or have dependants whose lot might be adversely affected by carelessness on our part. It is true that we are advised to "take no anxious thought for the morrow" (Matt. 6. 34), but that applies to anxiety about ourselves. The Bible leaves us in no doubt about our responsibility for our dependants. "If any provide not for his own, and specially for those of his own house, he hath denied the faith, and is worse than an infidel" (1 Tim. 5. 8). Our Prayer Book service for the Visitation of the Sick directs the minister to admonish the sick person "to make his Will, and to declare his debts, what he oweth and what is owing to him". But it also adds, "men should often be put in remembrance to take order for the settling of their temporal estates, whilst they are in health". Provision for our loved ones in case of our death is our obvious responsibility, but the importance of making clear by means of a Will how we wish them to benefit is often forgotten. Failure to do so could, in certain circumstances mean, for example, that a wife might not receive the whole of her husband's estate. He would be grieved to think that his failure had resulted in hardship for his wife. It is not essential that a Will should be drawn up by a solicitor, but it is wise to have legal advice, because ignorance of the proper wording can deprive the legatee of all or part of the bequest.

It is also important that we should give full information about our affairs. A wife often leaves all business matters entirely to her husband. If he is suddenly taken, she is faced with complicated business to transact, perhaps in complete ignorance as to how to set about it or where to find his papers. He should therefore provide for her in writing the fullest and clearest

F

directions as to his assets, the amount of his investments, and where the Stock Certificates are to be found; details of insurance policies, the value of his house and the location of the Deeds, and particulars of Post Office or other Savings. Any liabilities other than those incurred in the normal course of running a household should be stated. There should also be advice as to where his will is to be found and where his keys are kept.

There is a further very homely admonition. We all love to accumulate clothing, papers, books, and knick-knacks. The disposal of these things can be a sad and wearisome task for our loved ones. Therefore it is kind, especially as we grow older, to look them over from time to time, to destroy what is useless, and to dispose of what is needless, and thus make the task of our next of kin as light as possible.

In the prime of life we make long-term plans for the future, but as we grow older we reach a stage when the horizon of life is less distant. We grow accustomed to thinking of a limit to the years ahead and, if we are much afflicted by the weakness of the flesh, we may even look forward to death with relief. Some are called upon to face it before its natural time through illness or accident, and they need very specially the comfort and courage which God alone can give. There are some strong spirits who can face anything, but most of us tremble on the brink and fear to launch away.

Christians sometimes fail to enjoy the quiet assurance and the glad anticipation which should help them to face death without repining. A friend of mine visited a woman in hospital who knew that she could not recover. She was a professing Christian, but she was deep in a silent gloom, spoke little and spent her time in sorrowful brooding. My friend felt led to challenge her as a Christian. If she really believed that God had redeemed her through Christ and that she was in fact going to be with Him when she died, ought she not to be rejoicing in that hope and demonstrating the certainty of her faith to her fellow-patients? At his next visit he found an amazing transformation. She seemed, as it were, to have pulled down a blind over this life and turned her face to the future, forgetting the things which were behind and looking eagerly forward to the prize of her high calling in Jesus Christ. Her radiant happiness made a great impression upon doctors, nurses, and patients, and was a more powerful witness to her Christian faith than the most eloquent of sermons.

DEATH NEED NOT BE FEARED

We are afraid of death not only because of the sadness of parting with all that has made this life so good, but also because the act of dying is a new experience which we associate with distress and anguish. But those who are constantly brought into touch with death assure us that such fears are needless. An eminent American doctor says, "Death is almost always preceded by a willingness to die. I have never seen it otherwise. It is always easy at the last. However great the previous suffering, there is always an interval of perfect peace and often ecstasy before death." A French doctor writes, "Everything goes to show that God, in His pity for human weakness, has granted to most men a common deliverance in that they do not anticipate death. . . . To some He has given a particular sign of His grace: together with their realisation of approaching death, the faith or courage necessary to face it in peace."

A great saint visited me on his ninetieth birthday and talked quite naturally about his own funeral service and what he wished to happen, but his talk was for the most part about the joys of the life to come.

Countless men and women have found comfort in

the beautiful words of the Shepherd psalm (Psalm 23), and especially in verse 4: "Yea, though I walk through the valley of the shadow of death, I will fear no evil; for thou art with me; thy rod and thy staff they comfort me." The Eastern shepherd always leads his sheep; he never drives them. He guides them from one pasture to another in search of green herbage and still waters. The journey sometimes takes them through a dark and sombre ravine. The sheep cannot see the way, but they follow the shepherd with confidence, and as they look upward they see his form silhouetted against the sky with rod and staff over each shoulder. The rod is the heavy club with which the shepherd defends the sheep against its enemies, and the staff is the crook with which he rescues the sheep from a place of danger and draws it to himself. "Thou art with me, thy rod and thy staff comfort me." We have a divine assurance: "When thou passest through the waters, I will be with thee; and through the rivers, they shall not overflow thee: when thou walkest through the fire, thou shalt not be burned; neither shall the flame kindle upon thee" (Isa. 43. 2). It is this complete confidence in a loving Saviour which makes death, not a sad and inevitable separation from the world and its delights, but an abundant entrance into a new world where sorrow and tears are unknown; not the reluctant end to a busy life, but the beginning of a life of endless service unhampered by the failures of sin and by physical limitations. A young Christian who was dying in hospital whispered to me, "The sufferings of this present time are not worthy to be compared with the glory that shall be revealed in us". When the saintly Grimshaw, Rector of Haworth, was dying, Henry Venn asked him how he felt and he replied, "As happy as I can be on earth, and as sure of glory as if I was in it". When Henry Venn himself came to die, thirty-four years later, his lively anticipation of the glory to come so filled him with elation that it proved a stimulus to life. His doctor exclaimed, "Sir, in this state of joyous excitement, you cannot die!" Contrast the dying words of two men, one a noted infidel, the other a famous preacher. One said, "Now for a tremendous leap in the dark"; the other, "Earth is receding, heaven is opening, Jesus is calling, this is bliss. I must go!"

Stanley Jones tells the story of a missionary in India who was stricken down with cancer. She hoped to go home to die, but got only as far as a hospital in Bombay. From there she wrote to him saying it was as if Jesus had said to her, "Alice, that's enough, come over here and sit down a bit. I looked up, and there stood Jesus smiling at me. I went over and sat down on the grass by Him, and He said, You have been busy working and have not had time for all those intimacies that go with a great friendship, such as I want with you. Come along and let us walk together here! . . . Oh, it is beautiful. As I look down towards the river, it is a little misty. But I know He will see me through that. Even now I am forever with my Lord. His peace within me is wonderful. Nothing can separate us now. It is heaven. That's all. The doctors and the nurses cannot understand how I can calmly discuss my condition and outlook."[1]

How wonderful it will be to awake on the other side of death! We shall be "more than conquerors through Him that loved us".

[1] *Victorious Living*, E. Stanley Jones, p. 249.

APPENDIX

God

His Love. Psalms 23 and 116. John 14.

His Watchful Care. Psalm 121.

The fleeting character of life and the eternal quality of
His love. Psalms 90 and 103, Isaiah 40.

The ultimate triumph of His Kingdom. Isaiah 35 and
55.

Jesus Christ

His raising of the dead. John 11. 1–45.

His sufferings for us. Isaiah 53.

His resurrection. Luke 24. John 20.

His ascension and the promise of His return. Acts 1.
1–11.

Ourselves

How we may receive eternal life now. John 1. 6–14;
3. 7–21; 4. 1–14; 10. 1–18.

Our deliverance from condemnation. Rom. 8.

Our hope of resurrection. 2 Cor. 4. 11–18.

Our resurrection in relation to His resurrection. Acts
2. 29–36; 1 Cor. 15.

The need for watchfulness in view of His return. Mark
13. 24–37; 2 Pet. 3.

The importance of stewardship. Luke 12. 16–48.

Our entry into Christ's presence at death. 2 Cor. 5.
1–10; Phil. 1. 21–26.

The End

The events accompanying the resurrection. 1 Thess. 4.
    13–18.
The judgment. Rev. 20. 11–15.
The vision of the redeemed in heaven. Rev. 7. 9–17.
The new Jerusalem. Rev. 21 and 22.

PRAYERS

A Prayer of Confident Trust

"That ye sorrow not as those who have no hope" (*1
Thess. 5. 14*).

We give them back to Thee, dear Lord, Who gavest
them to us. Yet as Thou didst not lose them in giving,
so we have not lost them by return. Not as the world
giveth, givest Thou, O Lover of souls. What Thou
gavest, Thou takest not away; for what is Thine is ours
always, if we are Thine. As Life is eternal and love is
immortal, and death is only an horizon, and an horizon
is nothing save the limit of our sight. Lift us up, strong
Son of God, that we may see farther. Cleanse our eyes
that we may see more clearly. Draw us closer to Thyself that we may know ourselves nearer to our beloved
who are with Thee. And while Thou dost prepare a
place for us, prepare us for that happy place that where
they are and Thou art, we too may be: through Jesus
Christ our Lord. Amen.

                                        (*Bishop Brent*)

A Thanksgiving for the Departed

"Blessed are the dead which die in the Lord" (*Rev. 14. 13*).

We bless thy holy Name, O Lord, for all thy servants departed this life in thy faith and fear, and especially for........., beseeching thee to give us grace so to follow their good examples, that with them we may be partakers of thy heavenly kingdom, through Jesus Christ our Lord. Amen.

(*From the prayer for the Church Militant in the service of Holy Communion.*)

The Communion of Saints

"Who shall separate us from the love of Christ?" (*Rom. 8. 35*).

O Lord our God, from whom neither life nor death can separate those who trust in Thy love, and whose love holds in its embrace Thy children in this world and the next: so unite us to Thyself that in our fellowship with Thee we may be always united to our loved ones whether here or there; give us courage, constancy, and hope; through Him who died and was buried and rose again for us, Jesus Christ our Lord. Amen.

(*William Temple*)

For Comfort and Courage

"He healeth the broken in heart, and bindeth up their wounds" (*Psalm 147. 3*).

O God, our most loving and merciful Father; Thou hast commanded us to cast all our cares upon Thee; look in tender pity upon those who suffer bereavement, or any other adversity. Heal the broken-hearted, comfort the distressed and give them everlasting consolation and good hope through grace. Grant them strength to support them, courage to sustain them, peace to calm them, and confidence in Thy loving purposes for them; that they, being assured that underneath them are the everlasting arms, may be enabled to rejoice in the blessed hope of eternal life and to face the future with quiet confidence, through Him who loved us and gave Himself for us, Jesus Christ our Lord. Amen.

For Grace to be Ready for Death

"Blessed be the God and Father of our Lord Jesus Christ, which according to His abundant mercy hath begotten us again unto a lively hope by the resurrection of Jesus Christ from the dead" (*1 Pet. 1. 3*).

O God, who hast prepared for those who love Thee such good things as pass our understanding, grant me so perfectly to know Thy Son Jesus Christ as the way, the truth and the life, that I may come to those unspeakable joys which exceed all that we can desire, through Jesus Christ our Lord. Amen.

For Faithfulness in Anticipation of the Lord's Return

"Be ye also ready for in such an hour as ye think not the Son of Man cometh" (*Matt. 24. 44*).

O God, whose blessed Son was manifested that he might destroy the works of the devil, and make us the sons of God, and heirs of eternal life: Grant us, we beseech thee, that, having this hope, we may purify ourselves, even as he is pure; that, when he shall appear again with power and great glory, we may be made like unto him in his eternal and glorious kingdom; where with thee, O Father, and thee, O Holy Ghost, he liveth and reigneth, ever one God, world without end. Amen.

(Collect, The Sixth Sunday after the Epiphany)